DC 09 '02	DATE DUE		
NR 26 '03			.
1-19-04			
JA 19 '05			
NR 01 '05			
FEB 2 9 '08			
MAY 2 7 '11			

COSTUME, TRADITION, AND CULTURE:
REFLECTING ON THE PAST

Inventors and Their Discoveries

by

Richard Kozar

Chelsea House Publishers
Philadelphia

CHELSEA HOUSE PUBLISHERS

Editor-in-Chief Stephen Reginald
Managing Editor James D. Gallagher
Production Manager Pamela Loos
Art Director Sara Davis
Picture Editor Judy Hasday
Senior Production Editor Lisa Chippendale
Designer Takeshi Takahashi

First Printing

1 3 5 7 9 8 6 4 2

Library of Congress Cataloging-in-Publication Data

Kozar, Richard.
Inventors and their discoveries / by Richard Kozar.

   p. cm — (Costume, tradition, and culture: reflecting on the
past)
Includes bibliographical references and index.
Summary: Highlights twenty-five notable achievements in
science, medicine, and industry and the individuals responsi-
ble, including Alexander Graham Bell, Pierre Curie, and
Samuel F. B. Morse.

ISBN 0–7910–5163–3 (hardcover)
1. Scientists—Biography—Juvenile literature. 2. Inventors—
Biography—Juvenile literature. 3. Discoveries in science—
Juvenile literature. [1. Scientists. 2. Inventors. 3. Discoveries
in science.] I. Titles. II. Series.
Q141.K679 1998   98–33701
509.2'/2—dc21   CIP
                                                    AC

CONTENTS

INTRODUCTION

For as long as people have known that other cultures existed, they have been curious about the differences in their customs and traditions. Julius Caesar, the famous Roman leader, wrote long chronicles about the inhabitants of Gaul (modern-day France) while he was leading troops in the Gallic Wars (58–51 B.C.). In the chronicles, he discussed their religious beliefs, their customs, their day-to-day life, and the conflicts among the different groups. Explorers like Marco Polo traveled thousands of miles and devoted years of their lives to learning about the peoples of the East and bringing home the stories of Chinese court life, along with the silks, spices, and inventions of that culture. The Chelsea House series *Costume, Tradition, and Culture: Reflecting on the Past* continues this legacy of exploration and discovery by discussing some of the most fascinating traditions, beliefs, legends, and artifacts from around the world.

Different cultures develop traditions and costumes to mark the roles of people in their societies, to commemorate events in their histories, and to make the changes and mysteries of life more meaningful. Soldiers wear uniforms to show that they are serving in their nation's army, and insignia on the uniforms show what ranks they hold within the army. People of Bukhara, a city in Uzbekistan, have for centuries woven fine threads of gold into their clothes, and when they travel to other cities they can be recognized as Bukharans by the golden embroidery on their traditional costume. For many years, in the Irish countryside, people would leave bowls of milk outside at night as an offering to the fairies, or "Good People," believing that this would help ensure their favor and keep the family safe from fairy mischief. In Mexico, November 2 is the Day of the Dead, when people visit cemeteries and have feasts to remember their ancestors. In the United States, brides wear white dresses, and the traditional wedding includes many rituals: the father of the bride "giving her away" to the groom, the exchange of vows and rings, the throwing of rice, the tossing of the bride's bouquet. These rituals and symbols help make the marriage meaningful and special for the couple, their families, and their friends, by expressing the change that is taking place and allowing the friends and families to wish luck to the couple.

This series will explore some of the myths, symbols, costumes, and traditions of various cultures from around the world and different times in the past. *Fighting Units of the American War of Independence,* for example, will detail the uniforms, weapons, and decorations of the regiments and battalions on both sides of the war, along with the battles in which they became famous. *Roman Myths, Heroes, and Legends* describes how the ancient Romans explained the wonders and natural phenomena of their world with fantastic stories of superhuman heroes and almost human deities who could change the course of history at will. In *Popular Superstitions,* you will learn how some familiar superstitious beliefs—such as throwing spilled salt over your shoulder, or hanging a horseshoe over your door for good luck—originally began, in times when people feared that devils and evil spirits were meddling in their lives. Few people still believe in malicious spirits, but many still toss the spilled salt over their shoulders, or knock on wood when expressing cautious hope. The legendary figures of a culture—the brave explorers of *The Wild West* or the wicked brigands described in *Infamous Pirates*—help shape that culture's values by providing grand, almost mythical examples of what people should (or should not!) strive to be.

The illustrations that accompany these books have their own cultural history. Originally, they were printed on small collectors' cards and sold in the early 20th century. Each card in a set of 25 or 50 would depict a different person, artifact, or event, and usually the reverse side would offer a few sentences of description to explain the picture. Now, they provide a fascinating glimpse into history and an entertaining addition to the stories presented here.

ABOUT THE AUTHOR

RICHARD KOZAR is a former journalist and newspaper publisher in western Pennsylvania who now writes freelance. His latest book for Chelsea House, *Hillary Rodham Clinton,* was published in early 1998. He lives with his wife, Heidi, and daughters Caty and Macy, near Latrobe, Pennsylvania.

Inventors Remake the World

Without inventors, people would still be wearing animal skins and trying to catch dinner with their bare hands. But long ago primitive humans learned to fashion tools that they could use not only to kill prey but also to defend themselves from creatures that might otherwise prey on them.

Sometime later our ancestors harnessed the power of fire, a discovery that brought them warmth, cooked food, and security. Humans may not have invented fire, but they had the inventiveness to use this flickering tool to make life easier.

Later legendary inventors like Bell, Curie, Edison, Franklin, Galileo, and the Wright brothers shared a common denominator with prehistoric inventors: an unstinting curiosity about how the world works. Moreover, they weren't content with the status quo. Ever since humans walked upright, most have been happy to do things "the way they've always been done," whether harvesting wheat by hand or lugging the grain home on their backs. But one day someone decided there was a better way to move heavy loads, and that person invented the wheel.

For millennia, the only way humankind could record images was to paint them on a cave wall or, later, on canvas. Louis Daguerre came up with a better idea: the photographic camera. Once, the only way a surgeon could find a bullet in a gunshot victim was to cut and probe. But thanks to Wilhelm Roentgen's discovery of x-rays, doctors could clearly see a bullet's location before they lifted a scalpel. And if not for Orville and Wilbur Wright's 12-second flight at Kitty Hawk, who knows how long it would have been before people routinely flew through the air and into space?

The truth is, we owe our comfortable modern existence to the inventors in history, who looked at things as they could be and asked, "Why not?"

J. L. BAIRD

I n 1884 Paul Nipkow, a German, used selenium cells to record and transmit images by breaking them down into parallel lines of different intensities. Developing this idea, Scottish engineer John Logie Baird (1888–1946) is credited with building the first working television (TV) in 1923, when he received a patent for a television using an eight-line scan.

Three years after patenting his television, Baird gave the first public television broadcast in Great Britain using his new "Televisor." And in 1928 the Scotsman succeeded in sending the first transatlantic television broadcast from London to New York using shortwave radio signals, a year after Bell Telephone Co. demonstrated the viability of television in America by sending images over phone lines between Washington and New York.

Baird's Televisor didn't become a commercial product in the United Kingdom until 1930, and it was hardly snapped up by consumers there. It wasn't until 1939 that some 20,000 Brits had Televisors bringing programs to their homes. Although the French built a television transmitter atop the Eiffel Tower in the mid-1930s, and the Empire State building was crowned by one owned by RCA the following year, televisions didn't become commonplace in the United States until the early 1950s, following the end of World War II.

And even though color televisions weren't commercially feasible in this country until the late 1960s, Baird actually designed a color TV system decades earlier, in 1928. The first color sets had three separate tubes for red, blue, and green, but in 1968 Sony Corp. combined the three colors into one tube.

ALEXANDER GRAHAM BELL

Alexander Graham Bell (1847–1922) managed to go down in history in 1876 as the inventor of the telephone, but he did so by a twist of fate. Bell, a Scotsman living in the United States, filed a patent for his design at the New York patent office on February 14—two hours ahead of the patent design for a telephone filed by Elisha Gray, who had independently accomplished the same engineering feat.

Few other inventions in human history have changed the way the world operates as has the telephone. Today millions of calls circulate around the globe each day, all connected within seconds of being dialed. And since 1981 consumers worldwide have been able to place calls from mobile or portable devices known as cell phones, which use automatic switching systems to transfer uninterrupted calls as customers travel from one geographic "cell" to another. The result? Seamless and relatively inexpensive mobile communication.

All this from Bell's original invention, which managed to switch sound—originally just voices, but today data as well—into electrical impulses of various frequencies and finally back into sound. Gray had actually built his steel diaphragm/electromagnet receiver in 1874, but Bell beat him to the punch by subsequently designing a working transmitter sooner.

The legendary breakthrough came on March 6, 1876, when Bell, sitting in one room, said, "Come here, Watson. I want you," which his assistant clearly heard through a receiver connected to Bell's transmitter. Their efforts helped launch Bell Telephone Co., which would later become AT&T, the largest telephone company in the world.

JACQUES CHARLES

Professor Jacques Charles (1746–1823) is mentioned in the record books for making the first flight in a hydrogen-filled balloon, which he and associate Noel Roberts accomplished on December 1, 1783, by flying 27 miles in Paris, France.

The pair may have been inspired to attempt their historic balloon ride by the success of two other Frenchmen who had made a shorter ride only days earlier. Jean François Piltre de Rozier and the Marquis d'Arlandes had ascended 3,000 feet and covered five miles in the first sustained balloon flight by humans. Their balloon, filled with hot air supplied by a fire fueled with straw, had been designed and built by the French Montgolfier brothers, Joseph Michel and Jacques Etienne.

The Montgolfiers worked from an idea mentioned in 1766 by Englishman Henry Cavendish, who isolated hydrogen, the simplest element and lightest gas. He theorized that hydrogen, since it is lighter than air, could be used to lift objects above the earth. And since hot air is also lighter than cool air, the Montgolfiers reasoned it should work the same way.

Six years later Joseph Michel proved this idea when he filled a silk pouch with hot air and launched it gently toward the ceiling of his house. In 1783 he advanced hot-air balloons further, when he and his brother built a bigger prototype in which they managed to lift farm animals into the lower atmosphere.

The French were so taken with hot-air balloons they used them in 1794 during warfare to keep tabs on Austrian forces.

PIERRE CURIE

Pierre Curie (1859–1906) and his wife, Marie, discovered radium in 1898, at the end of a long and tedious study. Starting with 17,600 pounds of pitchblende, the principal ore of uranium and radium, they managed to extract only 1/28th of an ounce—or a single gram—of radium. Little did they know the element they discovered was a powerful source of radiation.

By the time of his marriage, Pierre was a physics professor already famous for his study of crystals. Also, while studying the magnetic properties of materials, he discovered that there is a temperature above which ordinary magnetic properties disappear. This is now called Curie temperature.

Working together, Pierre and Marie advanced the work of Antoine-Henri Becquerel, who had found in 1896 that uranium emits radiation spontaneously. Marie called the phenomenon "radioactivity." In 1903, along with Becquerel, the couple received the Nobel Prize in physics for their discovery of radiation.

Earlier, while attending a dinner party in Paris, Pierre and Marie were anxious to show off their discovery. In front of the assembled guests, Pierre pulled out a glowing tube filled with liquid, which he had kept in his pocket. The glass tube contained radium in solution and was coated with zinc sulfide, which was glowing brilliantly—fluorescing—in the darkness. Although a compelling demonstration of radioactivity's power, the display also revealed radium's peril: Pierre's hands were inflamed from holding the radioactive cocktail.

When Pierre died after being hit by a truck on a street in Paris, Marie focused her grief on continuing the scientific work they had begun together.

LOUIS-JACQUES DAGUERRE

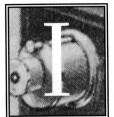I n the 1840s Louis-Jacques Daguerre's name was synonymous with photography, even though he was not the first to produce a photograph. That honor belongs to his partner, Joseph-Nicephore Niepce, who, sometime in 1827, managed to produce the faint image of a French courtyard on a pewter plate he had coated with light-sensitive asphalt. The process took eight hours, way too long for a "camera" process to be practical.

Realizing the need for a collaborator, Niepce signed a 10-year partnership in 1829 with Daguerre, a French painter who was also eager to develop photographic processes. Unfortunately, Niepce died in 1843 without ever making his own lasting imprint in perfecting a photographic camera, leaving the task to his partner.

Following Niepce's lead, Daguerre coated a copper plate with silver and placed it into an early wooden camera, little more than a box with a glass lens. After exposing the plate to light by opening the camera's lens, Daguerre, confident an image had been recorded (although invisible to the naked eye), "developed" it by applying heated mercury vapors to the plate and "fixed" it by washing the plate in hyposulfite of soda. He named the reversed image a daguerreotype.

The French government purchased Daguerre's invention, agreeing to pay him 6,000 francs a year for life and his former partner's son 4,000. When the new photographic process reached the United States, people known as daguerreotypists opened studios across the country, taking and developing millions of images a year.

SIR JAMES DEWAR

James Dewar (1842–1923) led the way in discovering how to liquefy gases as well as finding practical applications for them. A Scottish physicist and chemist, he managed to convert hydrogen gas—the lightest element in the universe—into a liquid and a solid.

Dewar is perhaps best remembered, however, for inventing a device that works because of the absence of a gas, liquid, or solid. His invention? The vacuum bottle, which is virtually identical to the Thermos bottles that today men carry to work, children take to school, and families carry to the beach to keep foods hot or cold.

Dewar's inspiration in 1902 was how to keep the milk in his son's baby bottle warm while he drank it. His ingenious solution was a double-walled glass bottle, with the space separating the two walls containing neither air nor liquid—in other words, a vacuum. This sealed, airtight space served as an efficient insulator, greatly reducing the loss of heat from liquids one would wish to keep warm—like baby's formula or hot coffee—as well as keeping cold liquids like iced tea from becoming lukewarm.

In addition, the inside walls of the glass bottles were silvered to minimize the transfer of heat by a process known as radiation. Dewar's vacuum bottle kept liquids stored inside at their original temperature for hours. Even so, his dubious mother-in-law knitted a woolen wrap for his original bottle, convinced her addition would ensure that the bottle really kept the baby's milk warm while he drank it.

THOMAS A. EDISON

As was the case with many other inventions, several people were working simultaneously on the phonograph concept, but only one is remembered in history: Thomas Alva Edison, the man who also invented the electric light bulb as well as many of the other most widely used electrical devices in history.

The year was 1877. In France Charles Cros came up with a prototype phonograph consisting of a glass cylinder coated with lamp black. The glass had been etched with grooves by a stylus (needle) designed to vibrate with sound waves. The grooves were then transferred by a photoengraving process onto a steel cylinder. Unfortunately, history doesn't record whether Cros's device worked.

Meanwhile, in America Edison had come up with a similar cylinder, only his was wrapped with a thin sheet of foil and etched with a needle. On December 6, 1877, he made a recording of himself repeating the nursery rhyme "Mary Had a Little Lamb." It was the first time human speech had been captured and retained instead of drifting off into the cosmos. The cylinder has survived to this day. Edison called his first phonograph a "talking machine."

A later development in phonograph technology was the invention of the Gramophone in 1887 by Emil Berliner. His device relied on flat metal disks rather than cylinders and became the popular choice in America and Europe. Over the decades, the disks were made of shellac, plastic, and finally, vinyl. Today the modern descendent of Berliner's zinc disks is the compact disc (CD), though it works by a different principle.

BENJAMIN FRANKLIN

One of America's greatest statesmen was also one of its few notable revolutionary-era inventors. Most schoolchildren have heard the legend of how Benjamin Franklin discovered the conductivity of electricity by flying a kite in a thunderstorm. Franklin suspended a house key on the kite string, so that when a bolt of lightning struck the kite, the current ran down the string and sparks flew from the key to the ground. The only reason Franklin didn't glow with sparks himself, according to the legend, is that the section of kite string he was holding under a porch was still dry, thereby making it a poor conductor of electricity.

Lightning caused as much damage in colonial America as it does today, and no doubt took a terrible toll by striking and burning many stately homes and buildings occupied by our forefathers. Franklin's solution in 1752 was the lightning rod, a metal staff affixed on rooftops and connected by cable through the house to the ground. Franklin realized that lightning—and, on a smaller scale, electricity—followed the path of least resistance. If it could be safely conducted through a house's lightning rod to the ground, it wouldn't travel through the building's wooden frame and start fires.

One of Franklin's favorite pastimes with guests was demonstrating the phenomenon of static electricity. He spun a glass globe against a buckskin pad, which sent a positive charge through a metal knob and down a chain into a wine glass held by a guest. When the guest put his or her other hand near the metal knob—gasp!—a spark jumped out.

GALILEO

alileo Galilei, the Italian-born physicist and astronomer, was one of the first scientists (1581) to observe the relationship between the length of a pendulum and the time it takes for the pendulum to complete its swing. Galileo theorized that a pendulum could be used to accurately measure time, which had been impossible up to that point. It wasn't until years later that timepieces required minute hands; until then, the devices were so inaccurate they could be off by an entire hour in just one day.

Galileo discovered that the time of swing of a pendulum depended only on its length. For example, a 39-inch pendulum takes two seconds to complete an oscillation, or swing. His inspiration was the oscillations of a bronze lamp in the cathedral of Pisa. Galileo observed that no matter how far the pendulum swung, all oscillations were completed in the same amount of time. He was trying to use this principle to devise a better system for mechanical timekeeping but died in 1642 before succeeding.

Christian Huygens, a Dutch inventor and astronomer, is credited with designing the pendulum clock in 1657. His invention revolutionized timekeeping, which, despite various spring- and weight-driven clocks, had previously relied on sundials to measure their accuracy.

Galileo's observations weren't only earthly; he also had a fascination with heavenly bodies. He was the first man to refine a telescope capable of seeing the planets as spherical bodies in space rather than simply bright lights. And he discovered the four largest moons around Jupiter and the rings of Saturn.

ELIAS HOWE

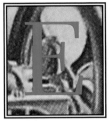

lias Howe's (1819–1867) contribution to the clothing industry was the lock-stitch sewing machine he invented in 1846. It employed two threads instead of one to make stitches. A Boston machinist, Howe was inspired to design his machine after watching his wife sew seams by hand at night to make extra money. His design concepts later led Isaac Merritt Singer in 1851 to design a perfected sewing machine geared for America's homes rather than factories.

Singer, also a machinist, modified Howe's design by patenting a rigid arm for holding the needle and a bar that restrained the fabric against the rising stroke of the needle. His machine was modestly priced and efficient, sewing ten times faster than one could by hand.

The advent of the sewing machine revolutionized fabric production, a process that had previously been constrained by the laborious and tedious hand-stitching required. The most immediate outcome was a boom in the ready-made clothing industry, which turned out to be especially beneficial to working-class citizens. And second, thanks to Singer's door-to-door salesmen, the sewing machine became one of the first American products that could be sold to a housewife for a small upfront fee and then paid for later in monthly installments. Singer's sales strategy was somewhat costly, but it ensured vast sales in Europe and America and made him a multimillionaire.

Singer later founded the Singer Sewing Machine Co., which originally made machines pedaled by foot power but now sells the electric stitching appliances found in American homes today.

WILLIAM THOMSON KELVIN

ord Kelvin (1824–1907) was a British mathematician and physicist who taught at the University of Glasgow from 1846 to 1899. He devised the "absolute" scale of temperature that still bears his name. On the Kelvin scale, absolute zero is the temperature at which even atomic particles stop moving. Kelvin was also a scientific observer during the laying of telegraph cables across the Atlantic Ocean floor in 1857–58 and 1865–66.

Lord Kelvin also redesigned the mariner's compass, a device used for centuries by sailors to navigate the seas. A compass shows direction, whether on water, on land, or flying above them. It uses a magnetized needle that tends to point to magnetic north. Typically, a compass's needle is balanced on a center pin and moves above a card depicting north, south, east, west, and the points in between.

But the basic compass that works fine on land is subject to serious interference aboard ship (let alone in a plane), with all the pitching and rolling a vessel undergoes. To compensate for this motion, a mariner's compass contains bundles of parallel magnetic needles positioned under the compass card, which swivels around its center in a glass-covered bronze bowl. The bowl is hung in gimbals—rings allowing the bowl to tilt freely in any direction. Suspended like this, the compass card remains level even as the ship heaves in the ocean waves.

The most stable type of mariner's compass uses a bowl filled with liquid, often a blend of alcohol and water. On ships compasses work well only if there are no nearby iron or steel objects, which can deflect the compass needle.

HANS LIPPERSHEY

Hans Lippershey (1570–1619) of Middleburg, Holland, designed the first instrument to make distant objects appear much closer. His device? The telescope, which he put together around 1608. (Another invention, the microscope, which made objects close at hand appear much larger, was also created in Holland.)

Although Lippershey is technically the father of the telescope, it was the Italian astronomer Galileo Galilei who carried the invention to new heights. In 1609 Galileo built his own version, which first magnified objects by three times their size and eventually up to thirty times. The earliest telescopes were simply a cylinder, capable of being collapsed and extended, with two refracting lenses at both ends. The eyepiece magnified the image captured by the farthest, or objective, lens. Later telescopes used concave mirrors to reflect the distant image onto the eyepiece, and they were even more powerful.

Instead of pointing his telescope at earthbound objects, Galileo aimed it toward the heavens, proving for the first time that the planets were actually spheres rather than simply distant lights in the sky.

And in 1610 he identified four of the biggest moons orbiting the planet Jupiter. In addition, his telescope revealed that Saturn had rings around it. He also studied Earth's own moon and came to see the mountains and valleys dotting its barren landscape. Unfortunately, Galileo's eyes also scanned the sun, a practice which we now know can be hazardous without adequate safeguards. The Italian astronomer eventually went blind from staring at the sun's spots.

CYRUS MCCORMICK

yrus McCormick (1809–1884) followed in his father's footsteps, figuratively and literally. Robert McCormick had once tried to construct an automatic, horse-drawn machine that could harvest America's vast fields of crops. For centuries in Europe and America, grain fields of all kinds had been cut, or reaped, by hand using a tool known as a scythe, which had a long curved blade attached to the base of a wooden pole.

As one might expect, the process was back-breaking, it required the resources of every available man and woman in harvest season, and it was time consuming. Unfortunately, time was a commodity farmers didn't always have in abundance, especially when bad weather threatened to ruin a crop drying in the field.

All the more surprising, then, that it took until 1826 for an Englishman, Patrick Bell, to invent an automatic reaper that cut and gathered crops like wheat and corn. Two horses pushed his harvester, which employed jagged, rotating blades. And only in 1831 did Cyrus McCormick, inspired by his father's design concepts, build the first mechanical harvester in the United States, which he later patented. Even so, neither inventor's harvester sparked much enthusiasm until they were displayed at the Great Exhibition in London in 1851.

Afterward the younger McCormick's fortunes took off, and his McCormick Harvesting Machine Co. in Chicago began mass-producing thousands of mechanical harvesters. At the turn of the century, his successful business merged with Deering Harvester Co. and became known as the International Harvester Co., which still manufactures farm equipment.

GUGLIELMO MARCONI

uglielmo Marconi (1874–1937), an Italian physicist, didn't discover radio waves; that honor belongs to Heinrich Hertz, a German scientist. But seven years after that discovery, in 1894, Marconi came up with a practical application of the budding technology: he sent a wireless electronic message over a distance of approximately one and a quarter miles near his home in Bologna, Italy. He was only 20 at the time he sent the signals, which used the familiar Morse code of dots and dashes.

Despite his success, however, he could find no one in Italy to back his research. He moved to England, where he was determined not only to build on his scientific achievements but also to profit from them. In 1899 he sent a wireless signal across the English Channel, and two years later his radio waves were broadcast from England to Canada's province of Newfoundland.

His novel use of radio waves produced an entirely new—and, in some ways, more reliable—means to communicate. Earlier telegraph and telephone systems were already in place, but they relied on a slim strand of wire connected from destination to destination. Should that wire be downed by a tree limb, or purposely cut, communication was cut as well.

Marconi eagerly capitalized on his successes, forming Marconi's Wireless Telegraph Co. in 1900. In 1909 he shared a Nobel Prize for his work. One of the most dramatic applications of wireless telegraphy came in 1912, when the ill-fated *Titanic* sent distress signals in Morse code as it sank off the coast of Canada.

SIR HIRAM MAXIM

Hiram Stevens Maxim (1840–1916) began a tradition of engineering in the United States, eventually becoming head engineer of the U.S. Electric Lighting Co. in 1878. However, in 1881 he moved to England, established his citizenry, and set out on his own as an avid inventor.

Maxim patented hundreds of inventions, but probably none more notable than the automatic machine gun that bore his name. Machine guns were developed for one basic reason: to provide continuous rapid fire for the soldier holding the weapon, thus putting his enemies at a distinct disadvantage. Since wars began, the less time warriors spent reloading a weapon—whether a bow or a rifle—the more damage it could inflict.

Richard Gatling, an American, invented the first practical machine gun in 1862. It was mounted on a set of wheels in cannon fashion and, when cranked by hand, could at best fire 400 shots per minute. In 1884 Maxim developed a gun that was fully automatic, continuous, and recoilless. His weapon relied on the recoil of a fired shot to eject the spent shell and launch a second round into the firing chamber. It fired 600 rounds a minute. The same year Maxim founded the Maxim Gun Co.

Interestingly, Maxim's brother, Hudson, also had a hand in things that go bang. He became an explosives expert and in 1901 developed the first smokeless gunpowder in the United States. Continuing the inventing tradition, Maxim's son, Hiram Percy, an M.I.T. graduate, developed several cars as well as silencing devices for everything from air compressors to rifles.

OTTMAR MERGENTHALER

Using movable letters on a press to make copies of a book is a vast improvement over the ancient method: copying manuscripts by hand, a process that could take years. Thus, the printing press, like many history-shaping inventions, changed the world by providing written words to the masses.

Bi Zheng of China is generally credited with printing the first document, in 1041, using hardened clay ideograms (Chinese word "pictures") arranged into sentences. His innovative techniques eventually became known in Europe, and by 1436 a German, Johann Gutenberg, had designed a printing press with movable type. His greatest contribution was to mass produce copies of the Bible, which came out in 1456. However, the type he used (metal copies of letters) was still relatively cumbersome to set in place and reuse.

It wasn't until almost four centuries later, in 1838, that a typecasting machine (pouring hot metal, usually lead, into letter shapes) came into use in America and then Europe. Because new type could be made very quickly, it was simply melted down and repoured into letters as soon as the current book or newspaper was printed. Even with this development, it still took a long time to set the type for a printing project.

The greatest advance in the field of typesetting was made by Ottmar Mergenthaler, who in 1886 invented a machine that first cast and then set type into whole lines. He called his machine the Linotype typesetter. It could set 6,000 letters an hour and was an instant hit with major newspaper and magazine publishers.

SAMUEL F. B. MORSE

Samuel F. B. Morse (1791–1872) was like several other famous inventors in that his technical talents and flair for innovation weren't immediately apparent. He was originally a portrait and landscape painter, a trade that helped pay his way through Yale University. Furthermore, he didn't exactly excel at academic subjects. Even so, he taught himself about electricity.

Morse believed he could send signals over a strand of wire using electricity, and in 1836 he had come up with a device that could do so—over a distance of 50 feet. He would turn an electromagnet on and off at the end of the wire, causing it to send pulses to a pencil that made marks on a moving strip of paper. By 1838 he had applied for a patent and was looking for someone to finance his invention. Unfortunately, he faced an uphill battle to gain approval and acceptance of his machine.

Meanwhile, in 1837 two English inventors, William Cooke and Charles Wheatstone, also patented and built a successful electromagnetic telegraph along 18 miles of railroad line leading from London. Morse, on the other hand, had to wait until 1843 for a Congressional grant to fund his idea. He ran 41 miles of wire strung on poles from Washington, D.C., to Baltimore, and on May 24, 1844, using the system of dots and dashes he had invented, he sent the following message: "What hath God wrought!"

By the end of the Civil War, 200,000 miles of telegraph lines crisscrossed America, and a telegraph cable ran under the ocean from America to Britain.

JAMES NASMYTH

ames Nasmyth, born in 1808, built machine tools and locomotives in Manchester, England. In 1839 he invented a steam hammer—a mammoth device used to shape red-hot steel and iron into various forms. By the mid-19th century demand was growing rapidly for steel, which could be made harder and stronger than iron and was thus a better metal for use in rails, which were being laid across Europe and America to carry steam locomotives.

Being a locomotive builder himself, it's not surprising that Nasmyth recognized the need for technology that could boost rail production as well as forge (hammer) larger sizes of iron and steel. His steam hammer consisted of a massive, bell-shaped iron frame that straddled a fixed anvil used to hold cylindrical lumps of hot metal several feet in diameter.

In the center of the frame, a hammerhead positioned over the anvil hung by a piston from an inverted steam cylinder. When steam was produced by coal-fired boilers and injected into the cylinder, the huge hammer could be raised and lowered with forces capable of pounding the steel below into ingots as large as three feet in diameter and several more feet long, the approximate dimensions of the paddle-shafts of steamboats. Or the hammer's might could be tempered to fall so gently it would only crack an egg.

Nasmyth's steam hammer was so innovative it was displayed at London's 1851 Crystal Palace Exhibition. And today modern computerized versions of his invention still forge steel into ingots in mills throughout the world.

SIR CHARLES PARSONS

he idea of a steam turbine first occurred to Hero of Alexandria in the first century A.D. He imagined how a hollow sphere could be rotated at high speed by injecting it with steam that could escape through ports, or exit holes, on the sphere. In the 17th century, Giovanni Branca wrote about turning a wheel by using steam that was directed outward against vanes on the wheel. The word "turbine" itself was coined in 1828 by Frenchman Claude Burdin, a professor who wrote about a new type of water wheel. *Turbo* in Latin means spinning top.

However, like many ideas that remain only concepts until transformed into practical applications, the steam turbine wouldn't become a reality until Charles Parsons designed a working model in 1884. Spurring him on was the budding electrical industry, whose generators required engines running faster than 1,000 revolutions per minute (rpm), which was the most steam engines of the day could manage. Parson's first turbine, on the other hand, was capable of 18,000 rpm.

In 1900 Parsons built two turbogenerators for a company in Germany. At the time, they were the largest and most powerful machines of their type in the world. But the electricity industry wasn't the only beneficiary of Parsons's steam turbines; three years earlier he had designed and built a turbine-driven sea vessel, the *Turbinia*, and staged an impressive demonstration for the British Navy. Powered by a steam turbine, the ship boasted an impressive speed of nearly 35 knots.

WILHELM CONRAD ROENTGEN

ilhelm Roentgen (1845–1923) was a German physicist who accidentally discovered a short wave radiation in 1895 that would forever change science and medicine. His discovery earned him the first Nobel Prize in Physics. While observing cathode rays in a glass tube filled with gas and charged by an electric current, Roentgen noticed that a nearby screen coated with barium-platinocyanide would fluoresce, or glow. This, although the gas tube was shrouded in a black cardboard box and the screen just happened to be lying nearby.

After experimenting further, Roentgen became convinced he was witnessing the effects of a penetrating, invisible radiation, which he named x-rays (because he didn't understand their nature). For a while the scientific community called the radiation Roentgen rays in their discoverer's honor, but today the term x-ray is used exclusively.

In medicine, doctors take x-rays to show what can be seen only by using radiation projected onto a sensitive film: broken bones, swallowed objects, and diseased or damaged organs. X-rays penetrate the softest tissues in the human body, such as muscle and organs, but are absorbed by denser materials like bone. In fact, Roentgen's first x-ray photograph was of the bones in his wife's hand. Shortly after this physicians used x-rays to pinpoint the locations of bullets in gunshot victims.

X-rays are also used in medicine to treat cancerous tumors and in industry to spot defects in products like steel beams. And passengers traveling on commercial airlines have their luggage scanned by x-rays, a practice that helps security personnel spot weapons hidden in suitcases.

GEORGE STEPHENSON

eorge Stephenson (1781–1848) succeeded not because he was an engineer or scientist but because he loved mechanical things and had an iron resolve that more than made up for his limited schooling. In fact, the man who became known as the Father of Railways barely knew how to read and write. However, Stephenson had an uncanny knack for solving problems, even if the solution required nothing more scientific than trial and error.

His pluck and skill earned him the right to run a coal mine's steam engine when he was only 20, an age when his peers were still digging coal. The engine hauled coal out of the mine, but teams of horses pulled the loads of coal on wooden tramways (tracks) to England's industrial factories. There was simply no faster mode of transportation in 1800 than horse power.

Stephenson was determined to find a better way, and in 1825, as engineer of the Stockton & Darlington Railway, which he built, he drove his steam-powered *Locomotion* down the 12-mile railway to prove its worth. The "iron horse" drew 12 wagonloads of freight, 21 wagonloads of passengers, and a car full of dignitaries.

Stephenson's next major project, which many believed impossible, was building a railway from Liverpool to Manchester. This railway crossed 63 bridges, two tunnels, and a treacherous peat bog. Doubts persisted about the use of steam engines until the confident Stephenson proved his mettle by building the *Rocket*, a steam engine that reached the then–remarkable speed of 29 miles per hour and beat all other competitors.

ROBERT STEPHENSON

obert Stephenson (1803–1859), son of famous railroad and locomotive builder George Stephenson, epitomized everything his father was not. For starters, he was well educated, graduating as a civil engineer from the University of Edinburgh. Although George felt he also needed an engineering degree to succeed, he struggled to grasp even basic academic principles.

Second, the elder, self-made railroad man was intuitive, combative, and insistent on doing things his way. His son, on the other hand, had the gift of working with people, even though he was more shy and retiring than his father. Together, however, the totally different father and son made a remarkable team. They knew how to design locomotives and the railways needed to carry them.

Robert worked closely with his father on the *Locomotion* and particularly the *Rocket*, steam engines that revolutionized passenger and freight transportation because of their efficiency and speed. But he was also making a name for himself in England and faraway countries, where he overcame natural obstacles with feats of engineering skill.

During the 1830s workers under his supervision drilled shafts deep into the ground and then linked them together one by one to build the 7,200-foot-long Kilsby Tunnel. After the underground tunnel became inundated with quicksand, Stephenson set up over a dozen steam-powered pumps that worked continuously for nearly two years until the tunnel was dry.

He also built the Victoria Bridge at Berwick-upon-Tweed in England, two bridges over the Nile River in Egypt, and the Britannia Bridge, a tubular-girder design in Wales.

EVANGELISTA TORRICELLI

talian mathematician and physicist Evangelista Torricelli (1608–1647) assisted Galileo from 1641 to 1642. When Galileo died, Torricelli took his place at the Florentine Academy as professor of philosophy and mathematics.

In 1643 Torricelli discovered why pumps draining water from mines could not raise the liquid more than 30 feet: the atmosphere's pressure was equal to the weight of a column of water 30 feet tall supported by underlying water. When he experimented further with mercury in a glass tube, he noticed that a column about 30 inches tall could be supported by air pressure. He theorized that at higher altitudes the atmospheric pressure would drop and with it the mercury level. Torricelli had invented the barometer, a device that measures the weight, or pressure, of the atmosphere.

Because the force exerted by the atmosphere is spread evenly through any liquid, the easiest way to measure the pressure is by watching the height of a column of liquid that is the identical weight of the atmosphere. Liquid mercury is still used in barometers, which are glass tubes approximately 33 inches high, closed at one end and open at the other.

When the tube is filled with mercury and then inverted, with the open end placed in a cup of mercury, the tube level falls to a height of about 30 inches above the cup's level. Changes in atmospheric pressure from a storm can be measured as a drop in the mercury level, which seldom falls below 29 inches. Although simple looking, the barometer is vital. It is still relied on for predicting weather.

ALESSANDRO VOLTA

An Italian inventor, Alessandro Volta (1745–1827), became the first man to produce a device that generated a consistent flow of electricity. He arrived at that discovery after initially experimenting with frogs. He found that by connecting two different types of metal plates—one wired to the back of a live frog and the other to its leg—he could cause the amphibian to go into convulsions. Unknowingly, he had created a primitive battery, generating an electrical current between two dissimilar metals using a moist frog as a conductor.

In the 1790s Volta experimented further with a more practical—and more humane—type of battery. Disks of silver and zinc replaced the metal plates, and he used felt pads soaked in salt water as a conductor (the brine is also called an electrolyte). He stacked the silver, zinc, and felt pads, calling each group a cell, and noticed that the more of them he stacked, the greater the electricity they generated. He compared the shock he received from the 40 or so cells to the jolt one felt after grasping an electric fish.

The Italian's invention in 1799 was subsequently known as the Volta battery or Voltaic cell, and the term "volt" (a unit of electrical measure) was also derived from his name. What Volta didn't realize, even after constructing his battery, was that the unexplainable flow of electricity, or current, was generated by the chemical reaction between the silver and zinc disks and the salt water.

ORVILLE AND WILBUR WRIGHT

Surprisingly, the Wright brothers began their careers as bicycle makers, as did several other mechanical inventors of the time. But it was gas-powered engines and automobiles—not bicycles—that soon captured the American fancy. And not long after autos began competing with horse-driven buggies, inventors began dreaming about whether gasoline engines could propel man through the sky.

However, the auto didn't require nearly as much inventiveness as a piloted, powered aircraft. The only air travel before the 1890s had been in hot-air balloons, a century earlier, and gliders. Orville and Wilbur, originally from Dayton, Ohio, were among those daring men determined to invent a flying machine. They experimented with string-controlled kites, then gliders flown by pilots.

The brothers had been inveterate tinkerers since boyhood, taking things apart just to see how they worked. They also spent many hours studying birds, particularly vultures, to see how they rode the air currents.

After years of experimenting with their devices— including a bicycle mounted with wings—Orville and Wilbur tested a motorized aircraft on the sands of Kitty Hawk, North Carolina, on December 17, 1903. Orville was the pilot this time, because days before Wilbur had slightly wrecked the plane, the Wright *Flyer*. Miraculously, the *Flyer* rose into the wind and stayed airborne—for 12 seconds.

The brothers took three more flights that day and managed to travel nearly 300 yards and stay aloft a minute. They had made history but received little press coverage at the time. Only four men and a boy were on hand for the momentous event.

Chronology

1581   Galileo explains the workings of the pendulum.

1608   Hans Lippershey designs the first telescope.

1642   Evangelista Torricelli invents the barometer.

1752   Benjamin Franklin invents the lightning rod.

1783   Jacques Charles makes the first flight in a hydrogen balloon.

1799   Alessandro Volta invents the Voltaic battery.

1825   George Stephenson tests the first locomotive engine.

1831   Cyrus McCormick builds the first reaping machine.

1839   James Nasmyth invents the steam hammer.

1839   Louis-Jacques Daguerre unveils the daguerreotype.

1844   Samuel F. B. Morse sends an electric telegraph message.

1846   Elias Howe invents the lock-stitch sewing machine.

1876   Alexander Graham Bell patents the telephone.

1877   Thomas A. Edison invents the phonograph.

1884   Hiram Maxim develops a fully automatic machine gun.

1884   Charles Parsons builds a steam turbine.

1886   Ottmar Mergenthaler invents the Linotype type-setter.

1894   Guglielmo Marconi sends a wireless telegraph message.

1895   Wilhelm Roentgen discovers x-rays.

1898   Marie and Pierre Curie discover radium.

1903   Orville and Wilbur Wright make a sustained airplane flight.

1923   John Logie Baird invents the television.

INDEX

FURTHER READING

Aasend, Nathan. *Twentieth-Century Inventors.* New York: Facts on File, Inc., 1991.

Amato, Carol J. *Breathroughs in Science: Inventions.* New York: Michael Friedman Publishing Group, Inc., 1992.

National Geographic Book Service. *Inventors and Discoverers: Changing Our World.* Washington, D.C.: The National Geographic Society, 1988.

Williams, Trevor I. *The History of Invention: From Stone Axes to Silicon Chips.* New York: Facts on File, Inc., 1987.

Yenne, Bill. *100 Inventions That Shaped World History.* San Francisco: Bluewood Books, 1993.